A CAT FOR 9 REASONS

MACKENZIE GRAFX

FOR ALL THE CATS THAT HAVE CROSSED YOUR DOOR

Hope this makes you smile and laugh when you think of all THOSE CATS

Vic Mackenzie
AUGUST 2009

Published in 2009 by Vic MacKenzie Grafx Publisher
Copyright in text and illustration © 2009 Vic MacKenzie

The right of Vic MacKenzie to be identified as the author of this work has been asserted by him in accordance with the Copyright, Designs and Patents Act 1988

ISBN 978-0-615-28135-3

Vic MacKenzie Grafx Publisher
39344 American Road Fallbrook
California 92028
United States of America

Printed and bound in the United States by Lighting Source.

All rights reserved. No portion of this book may be reproduced mechanically, electronically or by any other means, including photo copying without written permission of the publisher.

Library of Congress Cataloging-in-Publication Data is available.

vicmackenzie.com

Table of Contents

Acknowledgments	4
Nine things you should know about your cat	5
Nine steps to becoming a crazy cat lady	6
Nine cat rules	11
How you can tell if you are a cat lover	17
Famous Cat Hangouts	23
Nine reasons why a kitten is better than a baby	33
Nine reasons why cats are like women and dogs are like men	43
Nine things a cat does really well	49
Nine ways to call your kitty home	61
Nine cat breeds from around the world	62
The language of the cats' tail	67
Nine famous cat owners	68
Nine cat translations	77
Nine of my cat poems	78
Nine cat questions	87
Nine reasons why a cat is like a teen	88
Nine reasons why you look like your cat	97
Nine cat cartoons	100
Nine "whiskers" as a fashion statement	109
My cat Rhoman's Family Tree	114
Rhoman and me	115
Double takes	124
Cats and women don't pass gas	129

Acknowledgements

A few years ago my friend and former US Olympic javelin thrower Bruce Kennedy suggested I do a cat book. Rich Stergulz one of California's top portrait painters inspired and guided me with his brilliance. He showed me the light and I followed. His wife Lisa a true cat lover softened the book while Tori and Mike Brown kept me inspired. Caroleta Marsden-Huggins a moggy (cat) lover from Australia made some wonderful suggestions.

The main inspiration came from a cat named Rhoman. We inherited Rhoman when we moved from the city to the country. Rhoman was an independent free spirit who liked to live out doors. I built him a three level condo in a large ficus tree. He was a hunter and a fearless cat who was comfortable in his own skin. The dogs in the neighborhood gave him a wide berth and those new dogs, who fancied having a go at him, soon discovered a nose full of scars. Although getting on in years and now living indoors, Rhoman still controls everyone in the neighborhood including the humans.
A truly remarkable cat.

NINE THINGS YOU SHOULD KNOW ABOUT YOUR CAT

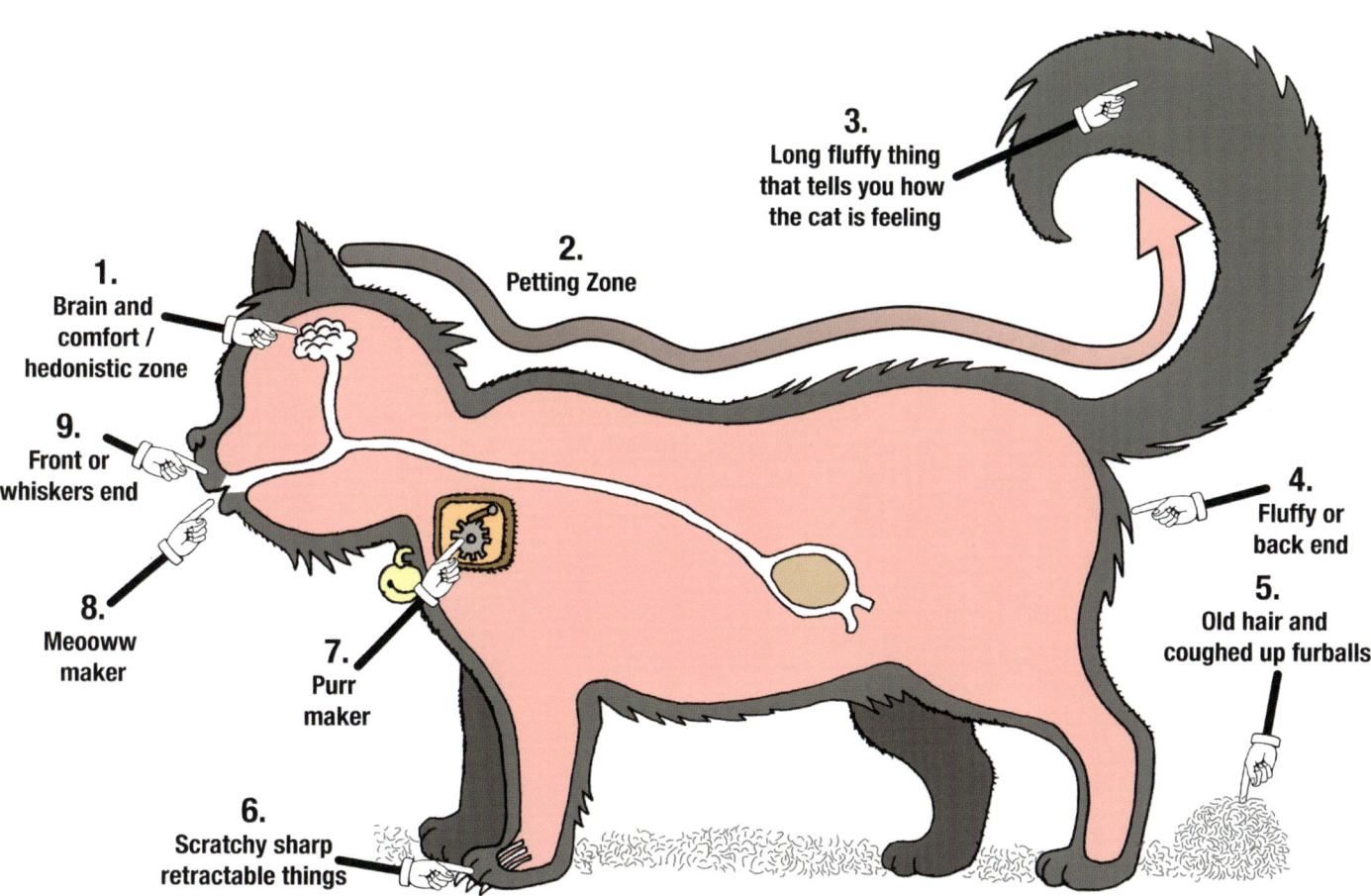

Nine steps to becoming a crazy cat lady.

Step 1. You start by pushing your cats around.

Step 2. Cats soon become your only true friends.
"OK, let's pretend we are cats on a hot tin roof."

Step 3. Love "Do you Todd take Kari and her five cats."

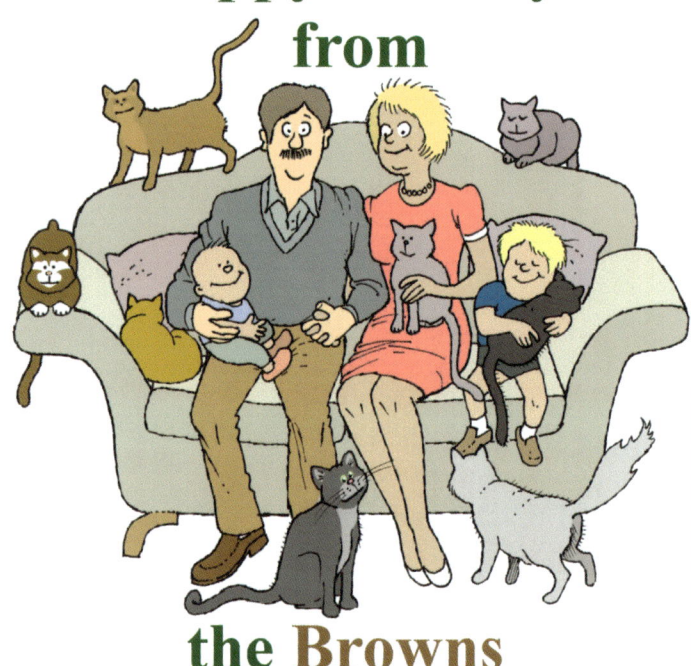

Step 4. Everybody loves cats and small children.

Step 5. "I don't have a headache tonight, honey."

Step 6. The ultimatum. It's the cats or us.

Step 7. Too many cats, too little cat litter.

Step 8. You rescue the cats.

Step 9. You end up pushing cats around.

The Nine Cat Rules

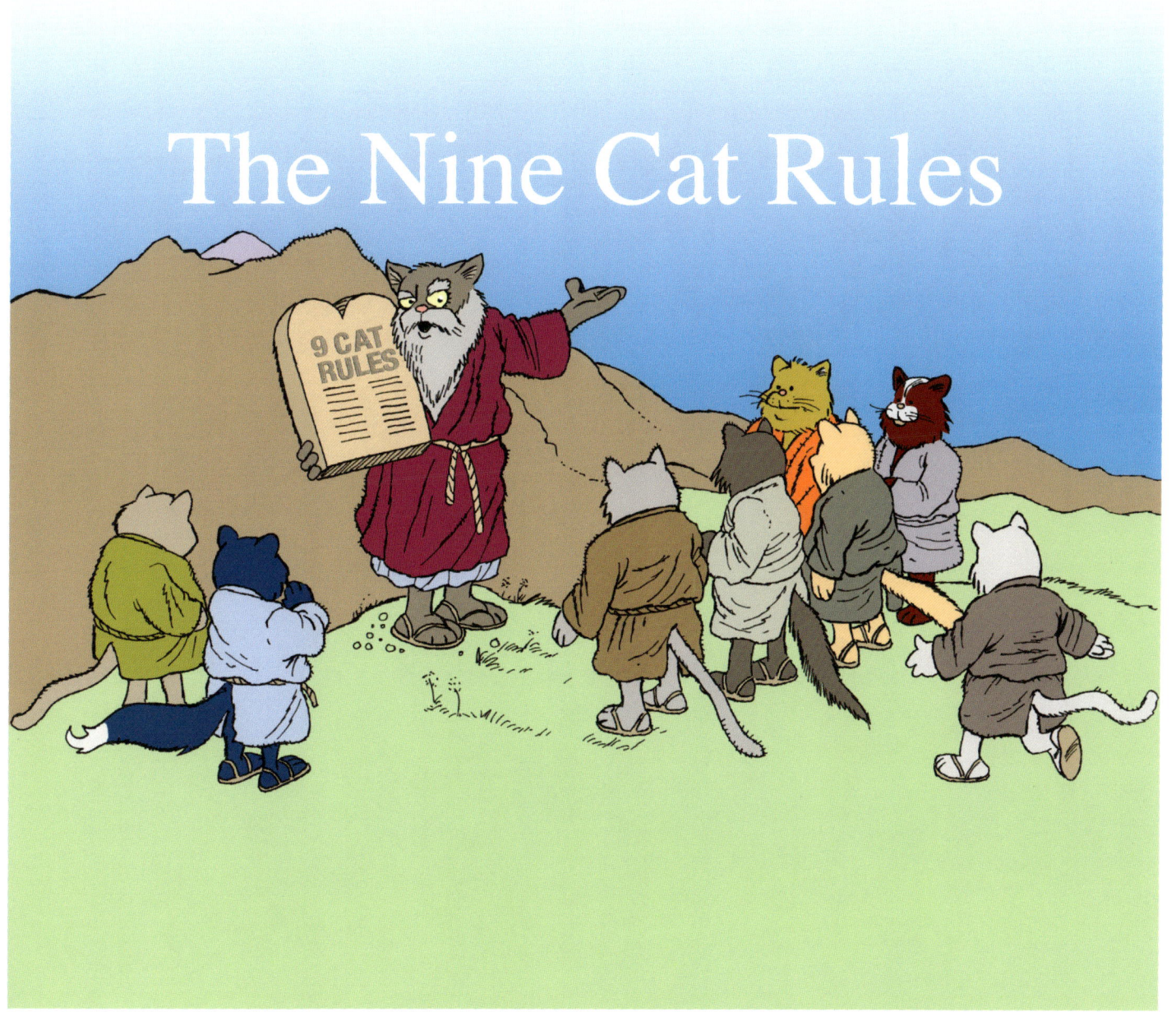

OK, OK, so we have these rules, but forget it, cats don't do rules.

Stretch and exercise your spine.

Act like a kitten once a day.

Bring gifts. Purrfect the art of giving.

Learn the art of the cat nap.
Practice daily.

Show affection.

Keep yourself well groomed and don't worry if your hair is falling out.

Hiss and spit when necessary.

Seek out the warm spots.

Hang on when things get tough. It will get better.

How you can tell if you are a cat lover.

Don't worry, he's just embracing his feline side.

You let the cat sleep on the bed.

You love your cat but can't come to terms with your cat being a killer.

You wear your love marks with pride.   You love the caress and greeting in the morning.

You always carry a lint remover.

You forgive your cat's untidiness.

Pictures of your cat litter your home.	You honestly believe your cat understands you.

You introduce your cat to visitors.

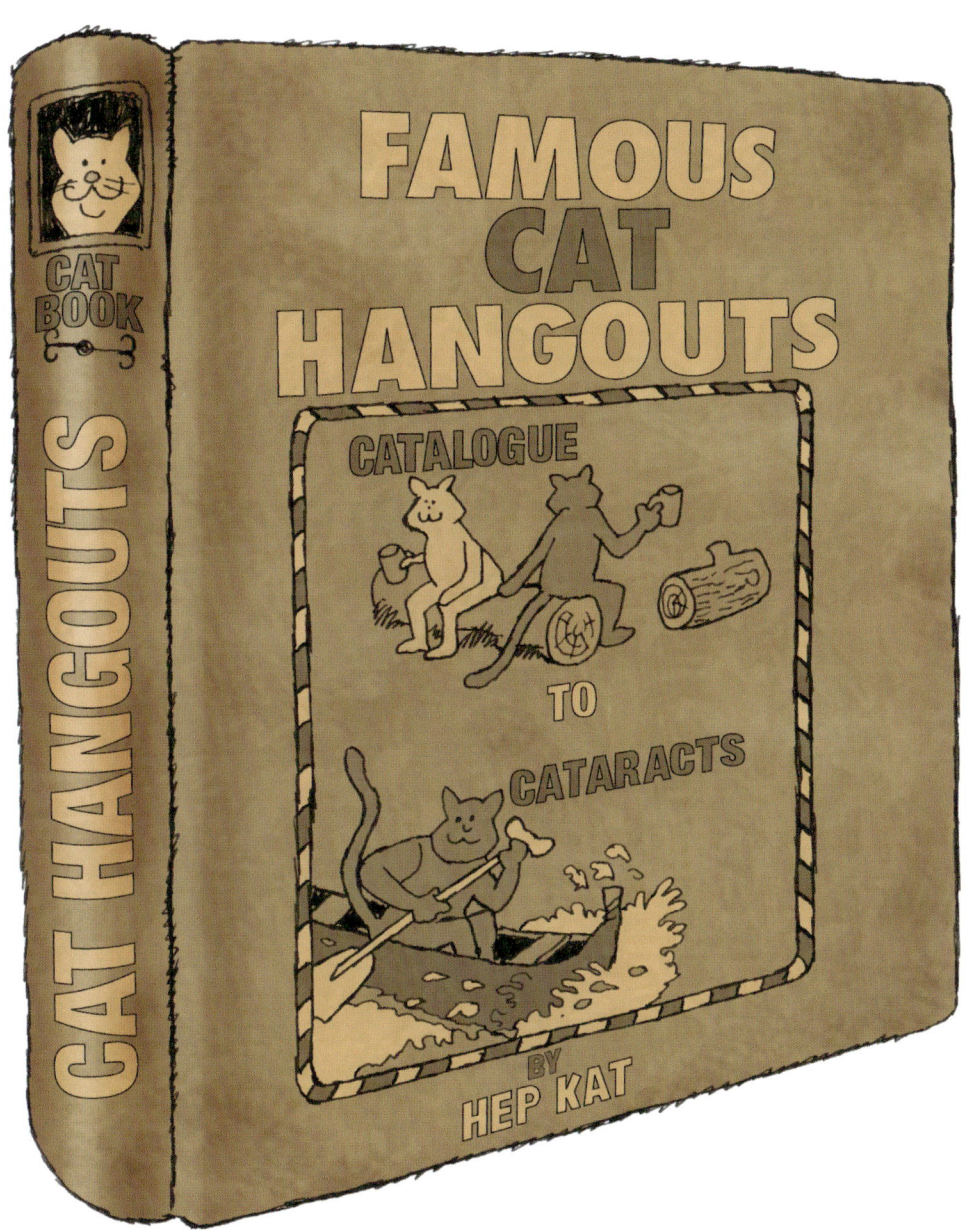

Corner of Catwalk and Wildcat Avenue.

Hellcat cafe.

Copy Cat Shop.

Cat-a-holics at the monastery winery.

Government Department of Bureaucats and Cat-as-trophy.

In-toxi-cats on Skid Row.

Fat Cats.

TechnoCats in the IT Department

Cat house
Reno
Nevada.

Nine reasons why a kitten

is better than a baby

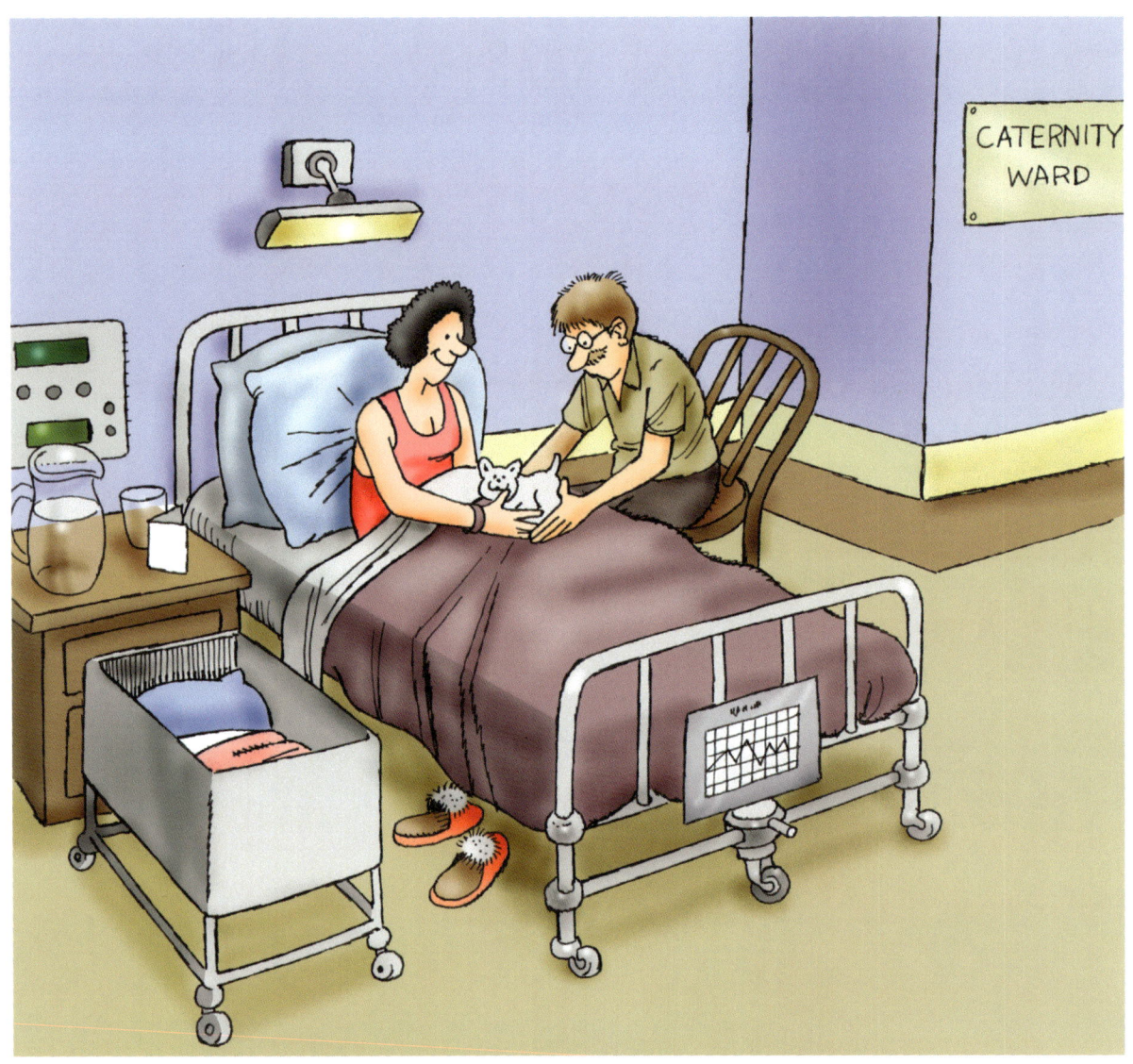

No pain or discomfort and a large selection from which to choose.

No paternity tests or waiting nine months for the little one to arrive.

You can leave the kitten at home without an expensive baby sitter.

College Fund

Baby   Kitten
$100,000 $0

No college fund required.

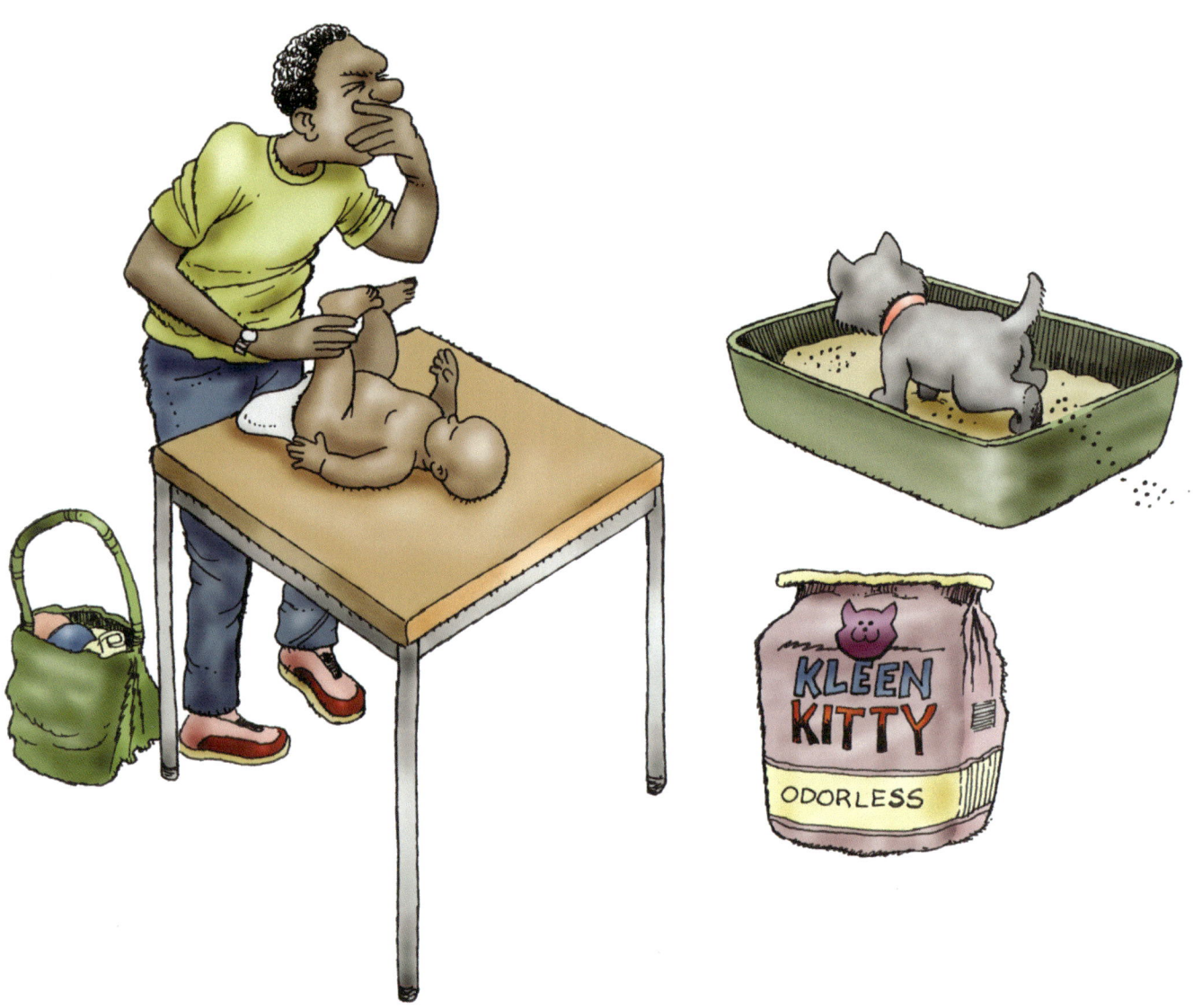

No diapers to change and your kitten can usually use a litter box within a month.

A kitty won't burp up all over your new suit.

Your kitty doesn't need constant check-up calls.

Traveling is such a breeze.

A kitten doesn't need expensive designer clothes, shoes and toys.

Nine reasons why cats are like women...

and dogs are like men.

Cats like to be stroked, while dogs like to be patted.

Cats are quiet and dogs are loud.

Cats will use a litter box. Dogs... er well.

Cats use their claws wisely, dogs just scratch themselves.

Cats whine. Dogs bark.

Cats have self control and don't pass gas.
Dogs will empty out a room.

Cats never admit their guilt.
The dog obviously did it.

Cats are neurotic. Dogs are simple.

"*Not now I have a headache!*"

A dog is always ready to play. When you are ready to play, a cat is NOT!

Nine things a cat does...

really well.

Sleep.

Groom at strange times.

Fall asleep in warm places.

Howl and scream late at night.

Go looking for amorous adventures.

Play.

Get between the feet.

Distract.

Have fun.

Nine cat puns...

and word play

Cat fish.

Cat of Nine-Tails.

Reigning Cats and Dogs.

Purrchase.

Purrplex.

Purradise.

Harmonicat.

Catapult.

Purrsuit.

 *1. Here kitty, kitty.*

 *2. Psssspt, pssssspt kitty.*

 *3. C'mon kitty kitty.*

 *4. This is your last chance.*

 *5. Mmmm hmmm, here is your food kitty.*

 *6. I'm shutting the door.*

 *7. Get your fuzzy butt here, NOW!.*

 *8. Bye, bye kitty!*

 *9. Meooww.*

Nine ways to call your kitty home.

Nine cat breeds from around the world

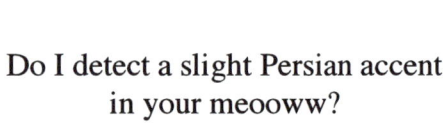

Do I detect a slight Persian accent in your meooww?

Himalayan.

Russian Blue. Burmese.

Persian.

Turkish Swimming Cat.

English Cheshire.   Siamese Rag Doll.

Scottish Feld.

Japanese Bob Tail.

The language of the cats' tail

Hi, how are you? Nice to see you again. Welcome.

I give up. Show me the way out of here.

I'm cool. I'm relaxed, nothing is bothering me.

I'm on guard. I'm watching you. Be careful.

Watch out. This is a warning.

I'm in defensive mode. I can scratch and spit.

I'm ready. Lets rumble.

C'mon over you handsome 'ol tomcat.

I have just chewed through an electrical chord.

Nine famous cat owners

Lincoln and Tabby, the first cat in the White House.

Mark Twain and Beezelbub.

The owl and the pussy cat went to sea,
In a beautiful pea green boat.
They took some honey.
And plenty of money......

Edward Lear and Foss.

T.S. Eliot and Push Dragon.

"We'll fight them in the alleys, we'll fight them in the litter box."

Winston Churchill and Jock .

Charles De Gaulle and Gris Gris.

John Lennon's cat Elvis.

Humphrey roamed the corridors of power at Number 10 Downing Street under Margaret Thatcher, John Major and Tony Blair. He died in 2006 at the age of 18.

Former President Bill Clinton and Socks.
(Socks died in 2009)

Nine cat translations

Nine cat poems

Meeces

I love to catch dem leetle meeces,
And tear dem into leetle peeces.
Watch dem squirm, watch dem flail,
Watch me catch dem by de tail.

Spring

*I love to jump, I love to spring,
I love to catch them when they sing.
I sneak upon them slow and quietly,
And catch them when they aren't quite flightly.*

Chewy the Cat

I often chew on tasty beef,
Sometimes I munch a lovely leaf.
But if I crunch upon a bug,
Watch me throw up on your rug.

In or out?

*Indecisions, indecisions at the door,
Should I go out or sleep on the floor.
Should I do this or should I do that,
Crickey Moses I'm just the cat.*

Cat on a Lap

Apologies to Dr. Seuss.

I never knew a cat,
That sat upon a mat,
Or appeared in a red striped hat.

The cats that I knew,
And there were a few,
Would sit upon my lap,
And take a quiet nap,

Until they had something to chew.

The naughty bed mice

Under the duvet's quilted patch,
I move my toes and start to scratch.
Slowly stalking, a flexing claw,
She jumps and bites them with her jaw.
Yeoww! I scream out in searing pain,
Her naughty bed mice have been slain.

The lady who had numerous cats

A voluptuous lady had numerous cats,
That took up space on all the mats.

They also slept on all the chairs,
The beds, the baths and on the stairs.

Her lover, her man, the light of her life,
Wanted to marry, and call her his wife.

Kitty cats scratched and started to shed,
And spread their hair all over the bed.

He sneezed and wheezed unable to breathe,
And broken hearted decided to leave.

Smiling cats glanced up from the chairs,
The beds the baths and on the stairs.

I lie on your face late at night

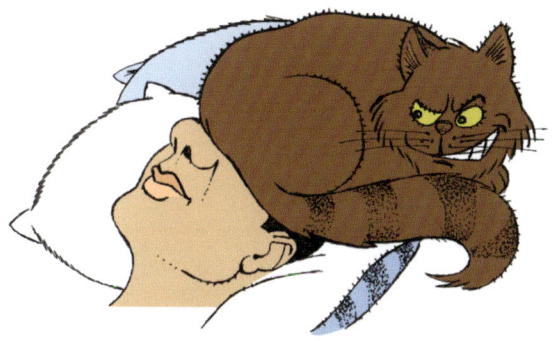

*Lying on your face late at night,
In the darkness not much light.
Flicking my tail here and there,
Watching your mouth gasp for air.*

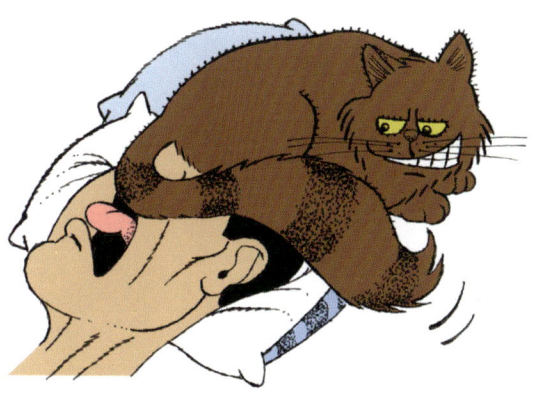

Fred the Cat

Cats don't do no fancy tricks,
But Fred the Cat could jump the sticks.
He could walk on his front paws,
From the kitchen and out the doors.

Jump through hoops and act elastic,
Do a somersault that was fantastic,
He learned to sit, he learned to roll,
He even could push along his bowl.

To perform these amazing feats,
Fred required lots of treats.
Before he jumped he wanted cheese,
If none was coming he would freeze.

Soon Fred became very fat,
And no longer was an agile cat.
He wobbled and gobbled and tried to please,
If only for that piece of cheese.

One day while doing a loop de loop,
Fred got stuck inside the hoop.
We pulled and tugged to get him loose,
To all it looked like cat abuse.

Fred threw up his paws and cried,
My tricks are over I'm now retired.
He lies around like other fat cats
Dreaming of his acrobats.

Nine Cat Questions

1. If "meow" is the universal language of cats, do cats from foreign countries have accents?
2. Why do black pants and black sweaters attract white fluffy cats?
3. Why can't you buy rats and mice in a can for a cat?
4. How come cats always take over the most comfortable spot in the house?
5. Why do cats always scratch the most expensive furniture?
6. Why do cats in cartoons never kill or seriously injure the mouse?
7. How can a cat sleep for 23 hours then spend one hour tearing your house apart?
8. Why do cats never do what you want them to do?
9. If cats have such a keen sense of smell why does their scent marking smell so bad?

Nine reasons why a cat is like a teen.

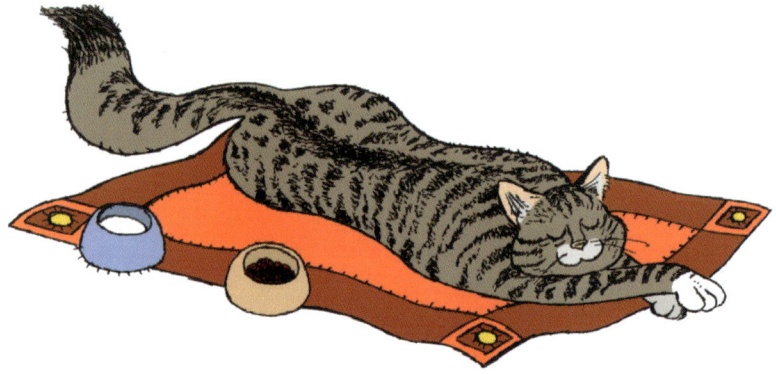

Hates getting up in the morning.
Will sleep all day.

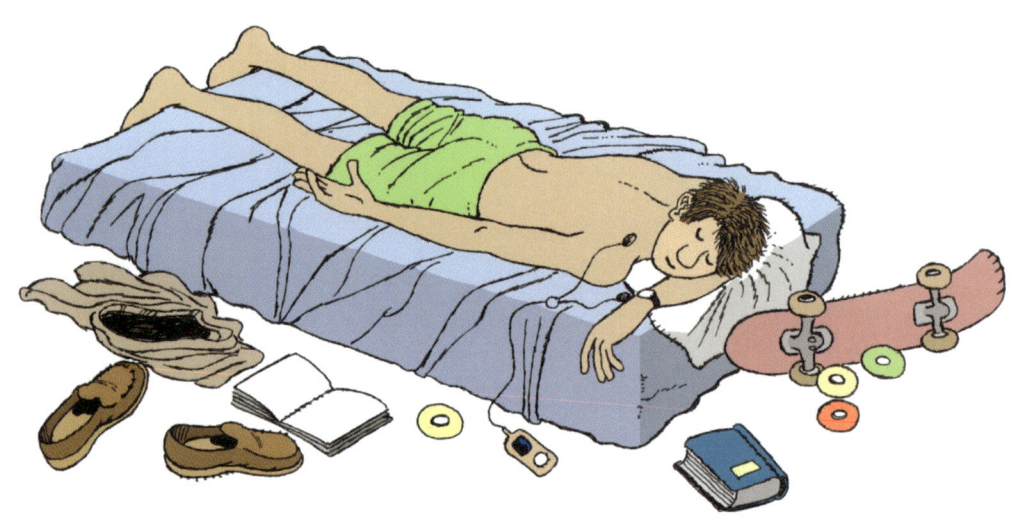

Likes to be fed, but is picky about the food.

Help themselves to whatever they fancy.

Will act strange and whine when unhappy.

Favorite sound is the popping of a can.

Will disappear for long periods but will come home, when hungry.

Call their friends
late at night.

Will become hissy when confronted by a higher authority.

Sometimes get stuck in precarious places and need your help.

Nine Reasons why you look like your cat

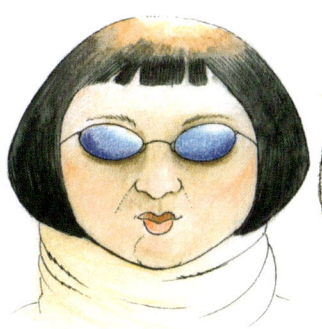

Your cat is suffering from the good life.

I hate it when he plays with these creatures before he eats them.

I'd like to get a dog, but this cat is something special.

Ignore him, he's trying to get the dog to move.

Mr. Katz, exhibit five thousand two hundred and ninety five.

Hope you like cats, they tend to shed a bit at this time of year.

Don't disturb him. Sit somewhere else for a change.

Aaargh me matey, we need to go to the pet store and buy him a scratching post.

Nine whiskers as a fashion statement

Light and Bouncy.

Military look.

Hip Musical Cat

Techno-Electro

Hang Ten　　　　　　　　　　　　Kung Fu

Mr. Natural   Walrus

Yin 'n Yang

My cat Rhoman's Family Tree

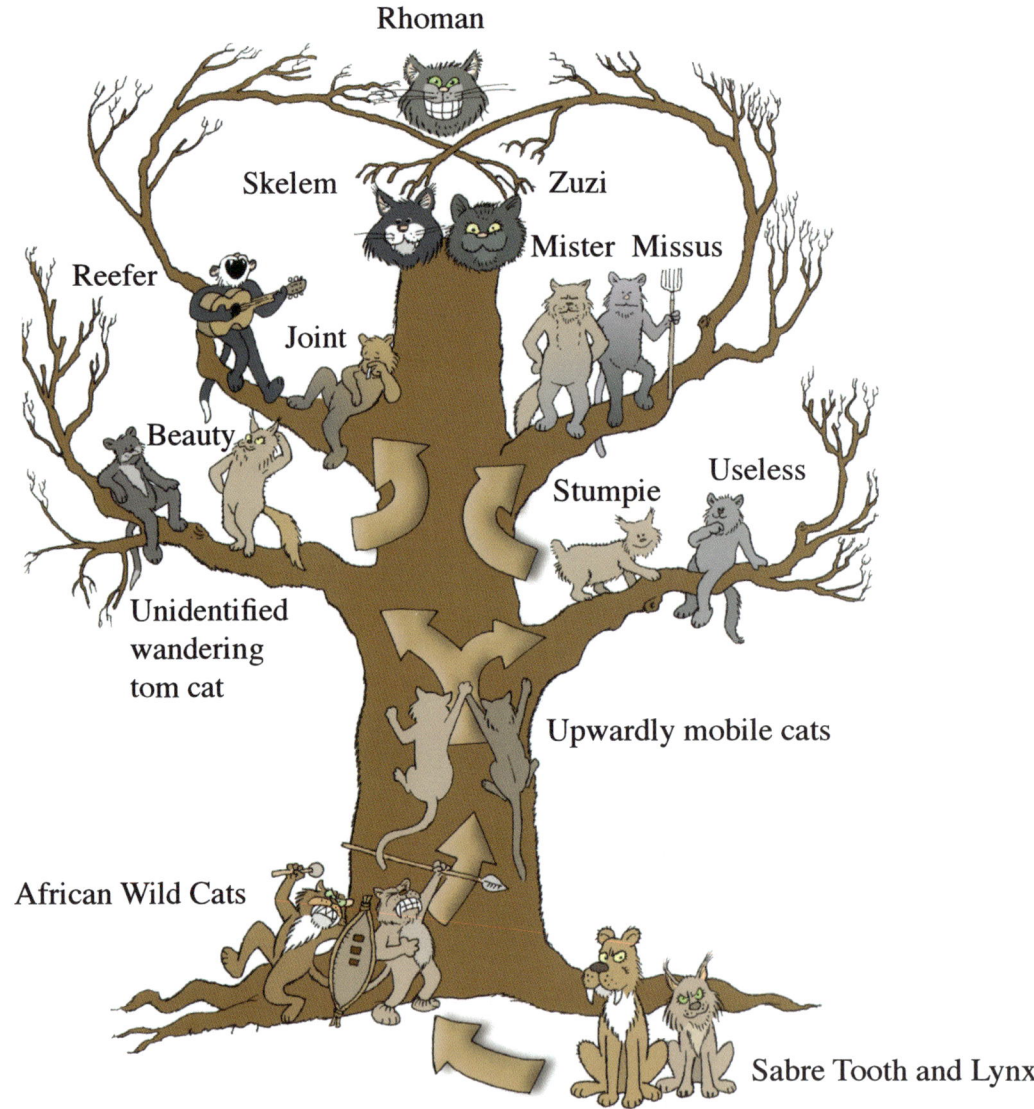

114 Nine steps to becoming Rhoman

Rhoman and Me

I have always been a dog person. As an adult I never had a cat in my life. We moved from the city to a house in the country. Part of the deal was to take ownership of the house and the cat. Rhoman was the cat. He was a large outdoors cat who thrived on the country life and loved to hunt. He had lived all of his years outdoors and had made his home in a large Ficus Benjamina tree in front of the house. We had simple instructions. Make sure he had his food and fresh water in a safe secure place and give him the occasional snack. That was it. I am not sure if he slept in the tree at night or on the patio furniture on the deck, one thing was clear he was an outdoors cat who had no intention of being confined to the indoors. Evidence of his hunting prowess was all around. Small heaps of intestines and stomachs of small creatures which he left drying on the deck.

My interaction with Rhoman was extremely limited. He had a complete distrust of his new owner and could sense I was not a cat person. I often used to see him lying in the branches of the tree and would have a very stilted and uncomfortable conversation with him. He was very suspicious of me and refused to greet me. We ended up tolerating each other and having very little contact. After all I was a dog person and loved the rambunctiousness of dogs that lived to play.
 Rhoman continued to hunt and patrol his large territory. He didn't need me and I didn't understand how he could ignore me. I gave him his food and water. Sometimes while in the pet store I would buy him a tasty snack.
This made no difference to our relationship. I figured if I put his food out each day he would be happy.

After a month, I began to feel guilty about Rhoman living in the tree, especially during the wet season in southern California. I built him a three-level condominium in the tree. It was completely weatherproof and fully carpeted. He had his sleeping area, a lush platform day bed and his protected eating area with an abundance of food and fresh water. The area was easily accessible for me from the ground so I could keep his food dry during the storms. He loved his new condo and settled in right away. He was now spending all of his day in the tree and hunting at night. Even though he had gone through a substantial upgrade in living quarters our relationship remained stilted, cold and almost non-existent.

The dogs didn't help. Every time he was spotted on the ground in the vicinity of the house, two very excitable fox terriers would chase him up the tree. The dogs would only chase him if he ran. If he stood his ground they backed off realizing he was a savy country cat who had been in many scraps during his life.

The change came when one of our fox terriers was attacked and injured by a coyote in the avocado grove. I needed to fence the garden in so the dogs no longer had access to the grove. With the wild little fox terriers behind a fence Rhoman assumed control of the property. He now felt safe and you could see his confidence soar. He had seen off one more challenge.

One day Rhoman jumped out of the tree and rubbed up against my leg. This was very unusual. I was eating a piece of cheese. Little did I realize but cheese was the way to this cat's heart.
I sat down beside him and shared my meal. Suddenly the mistrust between us had been broken. He purred and snuggled into me, but it was on his terms. He wanted a relationship but didn't want to rush it. Things were good but not yet perfect. When I reached out to him he was gone.
He had given me the first glimpse of only true warmth you can get from a cat.

Our relationship grew. So did our trust. He began to walk up to the fence and examine the dogs. The highly excitable terriers soon realized there was no fun in this and took to smelling him through the fence. In no time at all he had no fear of the dogs and was on the inside of the fence. If they got too close he would swat them across the snout.

Our relationship grew. He was now bringing me the odd carcass for inspection. He also became more vocal and I slowly began to get in tune with him. If he made a long meoww he wanted me to spend time massaging his body. I guess after many years of hard hunting it takes a toll on the body and a nice body massage does help the aching joints. The smell of a good piece of cheddar would have him rolling around in my lap. The conversion had taken place I was now a cat person. The cat had come into my life and touched my soul with warmth and affection. It had made me slow down and reflect on life and take pleasure in the simple things.

What made it special was bonding with an animal. It gives you an inner warmth and the feeling that the affection is mutual even though no words are ever exchanged.

Rhoman

Rhoman has now moved indoors. Age is slowly creeping up on him. He still hunts but not with the same vigor he did a few years ago. He spends much of his time out doors during the day, luxuriating in the warm sunshine and rolling on the grass. When the sun goes down and there is a chill in the air he hurries indoors. He now sleeps on a very comfortable cat bed with a heated mattress pad. He has adapted to his new lifestyle but if a mouse ventures into his territory his old instincts are aroused.

Nine Double Takes

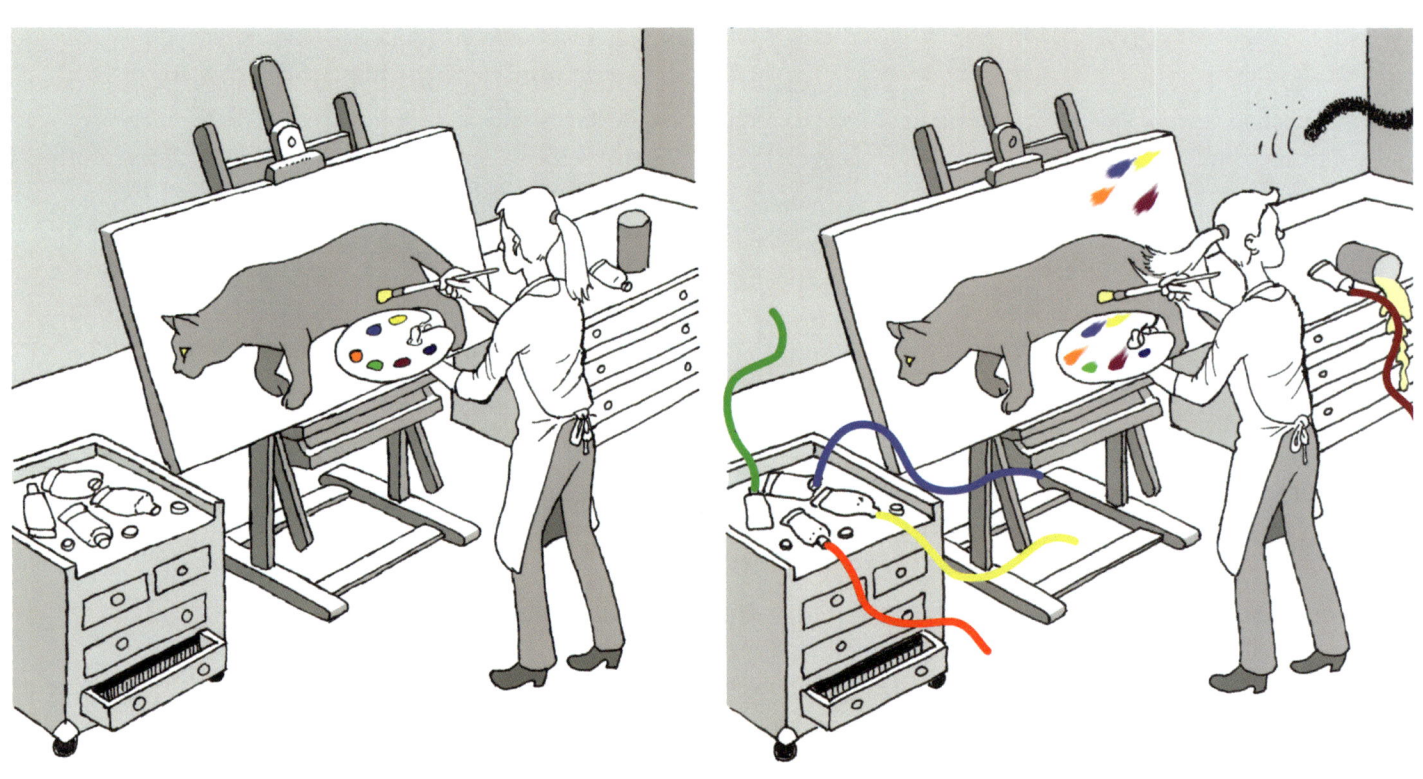

A cat has the ability to move at the speed of paint.

A fine white wine is usually served with fish or white meat.

However a cheap red wine is ideal on a sofa with two cats, a box of chocolates, tissues and a DVD of your favorite movie.

A cat has the ability to seek out people who dislike cats or have allergies.

One cat alone in a room is trouble.

Two cats alone in a room are pure mischief.

Cats and women don't pass gas.
If cats passed gas what would it look and sound like?

An extremely loud CATatonic cat fart that wished it was silent.

Aaah, this feels good. A CAThartic cat fart.

A foul smelling CAT Gut fart.

A very old and tired CATarrh fart.

A very loud CATaphonic cat fart.

A silent cat fart called a CAT call.

A naughty cat being CATulent and looking for a reaction.

A bad and nasty CATaclysmic cat fart

A very loud CATastrophic cat fart.

Printed in the United States
142166LV00002B